WILDFIRE

WILDFIRE

Homilies from the High Plains

FR. JIM SCHMITMEYER

ISBN-13: **9781537535180**
ISBN-10: **1537535188**

CONTENTS

INTRODUCTION

The grass fire advanced within a few miles of Childress. Sunday Mass ended amid the scream of sirens. Outside, dust swirled down the street. I stood at the door. Sand pelted my face like spit.

That afternoon, I rode on the back of a flatbed truck, shovel in hand. Smoke hung heavy and flames hissed in the grass. To the south, planes dumped plumes of water. Below, in the crags of a canyon, juniper trees exploded into balls of fire.

That day is seared into my memory. Now, years later, when I read St. Luke's account of Pentecost—its driving wind and tongues of fire—I recall that day in Childress.

Fortunately, the storm that tornadoed the Upper Room in Jerusalem outmaneuvers any fire on the open plains of Texas. The vision of the Dove that appeared that turbulent day is now mirrored in the graceful swoop of scissor-tail swallows and red-tail hawks.

Yet a counter-wind pushes hard in the country where I preach, eroding the earth and pitting the framework of every human desire. When storms bear down and shake the soul, I pray for courage and strive to preach the solace of faith.

A fierce landscape fashions many of my homilies. Some trod the rugged terrain of mountain trails, emergency rooms and detox centers. Still others delight in things as American as rodeos, truck stops and track meets.

Thank you for considering my work. I pray that the Spirit's Wind will whistle through the gaps between the words, redden the embers of faith and emblazon your trust in Christ.

Fr. Jim Schmitmeyer
Amarillo, Texas

WILDFIRE

*Jesus returned from the Jordan
and was led by the Spirit into the desert for forty days,
to be tempted by the devil.* (Luke 4:1)

His name is Steven Detten.
He's a rancher, farmer and volunteer firefighter.
Two weeks ago,
when grass fires roared across the Texas plains,
Steve and his family lost their barn,
their hay and their grain trucks.

Detten fought the fire all day and
came off the crew at midnight.
In morning, he located his seven horses beyond a draw.
They were alive, but barely.
They shivered in the wind with naked skin.
Their eyes burned shut.

Today's gospel takes us into the desert.
But what if it took us to the scene
of a wildfire instead?

Forty days of skin-scorching heat.
Burning barns.
Screaming horses.
The Lord's own face
smudged with soot.

In such a telling, Lent smells like smoke
and its sirens wail in the distance.
And the eyes of Christ,
like those of that rancher named Detten,
scan the scorched plain,
desperate to save the homes and lives of neighbors.

Maybe this Texas version of Lent
might compel the likes of you and me
to grab hold of this season
like a firefighter grabs a helmet,
      determined to dig in
      and stand against the destruction
      of all that we hold dear.

If Lent carried the urgency of a wildfire,
we would do something
about the meth house down the street
from the neighborhood school.

WILDFIRE

If Lent were a wildfire, we'd grab our Bibles
and head off to pray
with inmates in the county jail.

If Lent were a wildfire,
we'd fix up the house of an elderly neighbor,
or coach Little League,
or volunteer at the pregnancy outreach center,
or help out anywhere and everywhere
community health and survival needs a hand.

This year, on the plains of Texas, Lent begins,
        not with ashes on the forehead,
        but with soot on the ground.

And the memory of a rancher who lost his horses.

So, use his courage to energize your Lent
and stamp out the fires of sin
in your life and in your world.

Because that's the kind of action
that faith requires.
That's the kind of brigade
the Lord intends to lead.

SHE KNEW

For Susan McGurgan

The angel said to her, "Do not be afraid, Mary."
(Luke 1:30)

Mary, do not be afraid.
When Gabriel spoke these words to Mary,
they troubled her deeply.
The angel's message gave her pause:
Do not be afraid, Mary.

But how could she *not* be afraid?
How can any mother, or mother-to-be, not be afraid?

Any mother will tell you that fear and worry
fall heavy on the heart of a mother,
like groceries from a torn bag.

Do not be afraid, Mary.

Nine months of pregnancy means nine months of worry.
    Will my child be healthy?
    Will my child be strong?

Do not be afraid.

> What about colic?
> Jaundice, ear infections, speech impediments?
> What about school?
> Will my child have friends?
> What will I do when other children
> make fun of my child?

Mary, your child will be called the Son of God.

Maybe it was here,
at the reminder of God's promise,
that Mary stepped away from worry
and moved closer to God.

For indeed, a new life in her was conceived
and the Salvation of the world commenced.

But keep this in mind: it began in fear.
And the fear did not flee.

It tugged at her heart
each time the baby attempted to walk
without holding onto a chair.
And later, each time he ran from the house,
only to come back
with a bloody knee or busted lip.

Fear. It was always present.

Sometimes muffled,
like the sound of a hammer in the carpenter shop.
Other times sharp and loud.
Like the cries of the crowds
that would gather on the shore of the sea
to hear the words he would speak.

This son of hers, this child she cradled in her lap
now cradling lepers with open sores.

This son of hers.
            Going down to the river.
            Going out to the desert.
            Going out on the sea to pull in nets of fish
            with strong arms bronzed with the sun.

And she knew, as only a mother can know,
that one day bright blood
would stream down those arms of his
now so strong, but once so small.

And nails
would pierce the hands
she once washed with a cloth.

Because her son's words were strong,
much too strong.
And some day soldiers would come.
She knew they would come.
For him.

THE LIFE GUARD OF GOD

"I myself did not know him. But I came
baptizing with water for this reason,
that he might be revealed to Israel."
(John 1:31)

"I did not know him! Honest! I didn't recognize the guy."

So claims John the Baptist in today's gospel.
He says it once then,
a couple verses later,
he says it again:
"I'm telling you, I didn't know it was *him*!"

Now, this is amazing.
The reason John
went out to the desert,
lived on insects,
and preached until his voice turned hoarse
—the very reason he was born—
       was to *Prepare the way!*
       Proclaim the Messiah!
       Pump up the people!

And now we get this?
"Sorry, folks, I didn't expect him at the river."

But then, suddenly, he recognizes Christ,
the Messiah,
standing in line with the sinners,
knee-deep in mud on the bank of the Jordan.

Their eyes meet and John shouts,
"Look, the Lamb of God!"
And our response is, "So?"

Unless we know the history of Temple sacrifice,
we miss the connection between
"the Lamb of God" and
"the One who takes the bullet."

Yet, that's what the term means:
the Savior *who lays down his life.*
> For humanity.
> For you.
> For me.
> For every sinner who has ever stepped
> into the mud and muck of life.

So, John the Baptist should have shouted,
"Look! The *First Responder* of God!"

Or, "Look! The Firefighter of God."

"The Lifeguard of God!"
"The para-medic of God!"

That is *who* the Lamb of God is
and *what* the Lamb of God does.

The one who puts his life on the line
to rescue drowning people.
>   Broken people.
>   People lost in the wilderness.

Despite all John's theological training
and personal asceticism,
all he could say was,
"I did not recognize him.
At least, not at first."

So, what about us?

Each Sunday,
the priest holds up the consecrated Bread
and says,
"This is the Lamb of God
who takes away the sin of the world."

What impact does that term,
the Lamb of God,
have on us today?

What if he were to say,
"Look, the *Savior-Pilot*,
    maneuvering a helicopter
    into the canyon of despair,

        sweeping the search light of hope
        into the deep crevice of cancer,

        lowering a harness
        down the cliff of family discord?"

Look, the Lamb of God!

A swimmer
        hurling a life-preserver
        across waves of oppression.

Yes! The Lamb of God!

The medic arriving with bandages
        to swab the wounds of betrayal
        and bind a splint to the spirit
        broken by addiction.

Behold, the Lamb of God,
the *First Responder,*
who takes away the sins of the world.

Behold the Lamb of God!
Behold him who takes away
the sins of the world!
       And blessed are we
       who are called
       to the Supper of the Lamb.

ROOM 24

When the angels went away from them to
heaven, the shepherds said to one another,
"Let us go, then, to Bethlehem to see
this thing that has taken place,
which the Lord has made known to us."
(Luke 2:15)

Listening to the Word of God
is different from taking notes
in chemistry class.

Nor is it like listening to a rock band.
Nor is it the sales pitch of an infomercial.

Rather, attending to the Word of the Lord
is like straining to decipher
an urgent message
beneath the jagged sounds
of a poor phone connection.

Close attention is required.

On a winter night
I drive to Northwest Hospital
to visit a mother and a baby.
The person at the front desk
directs me to the NICU.
The nurse at the station
directs me to Room 24.

As soon as I enter room, I realize the mistake.
I find myself staring at three strangers:
a young mother, a young father
and a newborn struggling to breathe.

"Excuse me," I say. "I'm in the wrong room."

The mother, too young to be married,
holds the baby on her lap.
The father is also a teenager.
Skinny.
Tattoos on his arms.
Rings in his nose.
And probably no job.

And I'm thinking to myself, *Loser.*

The mother fixes her gaze on the baby.
I catch the young man's eye.
For a moment, we stare at each other.

Then he says something I do not expect:
"Father, we could use some prayers."

So I kneel on the floor to bless the baby.
Suddenly,
I am in the presence of another young couple
who didn't have much of a place in this world.

There, amid plastic tubes
and the murmur of medical equipment,
I hear a song.

Angels singing.
Singing glory to God.
Glory to God in the Highest.

VISIBLE AND INVISIBLE

"We saw his star at its rising
and have come to do him homage."
(Matthew 2:2)

On a clear October night,
a friend leaves a message on my phone:
"Look to the east, just above the horizon.
You'll see Venus, Jupiter and Mars in a straight line."

I open the door and walk out on the porch.
Sure enough, I see three bright stars,
straight as an arrow,
pointing from Earth to Heaven.

Today is the Feast of the Epiphany,
and we hear the story about a star in the heavens
pointing straight to the Son of God,
the Savior of the world.

Some preachers will focus on the mysterious Magi,
or their exotic gifts.
But this year, your preacher is going to focus on the star.

Was there an actual star?
Or is the star just a symbol? A literary device?

For centuries, astronomers and scripture scholars
have endeavored to answer these questions.
Why?
Because, if the detail about the star is true,
it's more likely that the entire story
—the story of humanity's Salvation—
is also true.

Is it true?
We all want to know,
Is it true?

But first, another question:
Are you familiar with the term, exoplanets?
An exoplanet is a planet
that no astronomer has ever seen
but knows exists.

Exoplanets are located outside our solar system
and orbit stars similar to our sun.
How does a scientist discover an exoplanet?
Not by looking through a telescope and saying,
"Aha! There it is! I've spotted an exoplanet!"

Rather, the astronomer
focuses on the star
and the periodic changes in the light
that comes from that star,
changes caused by the orbiting exoplanet,
which our instruments
are not yet capable of actually spotting.

So, if you look for an exoplanet,
you'll never find one.
Instead, you must focus
on the slight changes in the brilliance of a star.
Those changes tell us
that there is something orbiting that star
on a regular, predictable basis.
That "something" is an exoplanet.

No one has seen an exoplanet,
but we know they exist.

My point is this:
scientists do not hesitate
to acknowledge invisible realities
when such realities
make things make more sense.

The same rule is applied in theology.
In the Nicene Creed,

Christians profess faith
in *things visible and invisible,* including God.
We don't *really know* if God exists but,
based on our observations,
we can draw certain conclusions.

Likewise, we don't really know
if the star of Bethlehem literally existed.
Nevertheless, we remain open to belief
in *things invisible.*

Keep your eye peeled
for more than meets the eye!

The day after Christmas,
a friend called to tell me
that he prayed a novena
for his twelve-year-old daughter.

My friend is divorced and his daughter lives far away.
He loves his daughter very much
and visits her on a regular basis.
But he grieves the fact
that he cannot have a steady presence
in her day-to-day life.

Back in November,
prior to the Feast of the Immaculate Conception,

he prayed a rosary each day,
asking Our Lady to intercede for his daughter.

He also asked for something more.
He asked Blessed Mary
to give him a sign.

On the last day of the novena,
when he left his house
to attend his daughter's dance recital,
a rose was blooming in the flowerbed.

This occurred in the first week of December.

Now, we enjoyed unusually warm days
in the Texas Panhandle this winter.
Yet, on this bush, there was just one rose.
Just a single rose.
No other roses had bloomed.

My friend reached down, plucked that rose
and gave it to his daughter after the recital.
But kept one petal back.

On Christmas,
he presented his daughter with a gold locket.
And inside that locket
was a petal from that rose.

Did Mary actually cause that rose to bloom?

Such a question misses the point of the story.
Because it misses the *meaning* of the story.

When we consider its meaning,
we discover a deep truth,
a truth that is deeper than weather patterns.

We uncover the truth about the love
of a father for his daughter.

The writer, C.S. Lewis,
a convert from atheism,
once said,
"I believe in Christianity
the same way that I believe in the sun in the sky.
I believe in the sun
not only because it has risen,
but because, by the light of that sun,
I am able to see everything else."

In today's gospel story, a star led the Magi to Christ.
In the life of my friend,
a rose petal is leading his daughter to Mary
who, in turn, will lead his daughter
to her Son.

Like scientists, we believe in exoplanets.
Like separated parents,
we trust in the reality
of long distance love.

We believe in things visible.
And invisible.

We search the skies
and search our lives
        for stars and planets
        and roses in winter.

        To point us to God.

        To point us straight to God.

"I THIRST"

A woman of Samaria came to draw water.
Jesus said to her, "Give me a drink."
(John 4:7)

The woman who came to the well to draw
water represents every person who has ever felt thirst.

In particular, the thirst for God.

In this story,
Jesus also experiences thirst.

Later on, in the same gospel,
St. John again draws our attention
to Jesus' thirst.

He notes that one of the last phrases
Christ utters on the cross is,
"I thirst."

The torture that Jesus endured
would have resulted in extreme thirst
in the final moments of his life.

According to Matthew's gospel,
a rag soaked in vinegar
was hoisted to Jesus' lips to satisfy that thirst.

The writer, Elizabeth Duffy,
reflects on this detail of the Lord's passion
and suggests that Jesus' intense thirst
went unquenched into the next life.

She concludes that, in the death of Christ,
the Scriptures reveal that God himself
will forever thirst for humanity.

And how does humanity respond?
Humanity will turn away.
Humanity will refuse
to quench the deep thirst of God:

      in the weak and the vulnerable,
      the battered woman,
      the unborn child,
      the exile,
      the refugee,
      the elderly,
      the helpless
      and the poor.

This is the stark lesson of Good Friday.
But the lesson does not end
with the cry for water.
Rather,
when a soldier lances the side of Christ,
blood and water flow from the torso,
releasing the power of the Sacraments:
> the saving water of Holy Baptism,
> the redeeming blood of the Holy Eucharist
> and the endless mercy of Holy Penance.

> The Fountain of Life-giving Water
> flowing from the side of Christ,
> the only fountain
> that can adequately quench
> our thirst for God.

Today, at this Mass,
we will call forth
individuals preparing to encounter Christ
in the Sacramental Life of the Church.

> We will call them forth
> and we will pray for them
> —and for ourselves—
> that, as the Samaritan quenched her thirst,
> we too may quench ours.

Realizing that the One for whom we thirst
also thirsts for us.

"I thirst," said the Lord.

The world gave him a sponge soaked in vinegar.

We give Him our life.
Our very life.
Soaked in love.

TEASER TRAIL

*Take your son, your only son Isaac, whom you love,
and go to the land of Moriah*
(Genesis 2:22)

I have friends who hunt deer.
They don't read the Bible much.
But they're good at reading trails.

Most trails are easy to follow:
bent blades of grass in open meadows.
Such trails are traveled by does and fawns
as they hurry
from one protective stand of trees to another.

But these aren't the trails traveled by the bucks.

Bucks travel alone.
They seldom move out of dense cover.
They might travel a well-established route
but only occasionally.

Sometimes, they lay down trails that lead nowhere.

Hunters call these trails "teasers."
They lead nowhere but confusion.

Today's story about Abraham
placing his son on some primitive altar
in the land of Moriah
is a teaser trail.

You don't have to be a hunter to encounter one.

If you've ever clutched a steering wheel,
speeding your daughter to the ER,
you've been on that trail to Moriah.

If you've ever received a call at 3 a.m.
then drove yourself
to the county jail
to pick up your son,
you've been on this kind of trail.

I recall a night
when a young man from my parish named Sam
was stabbed and critically injured.

I rushed to the hospital and prayed with his parents.
All we could plead was
"Don't take him from us, Lord!"

Our prayers were polite,
the words respectful.
But what we meant to say was:
"Don't ask this of us, God!
Don't you *dare* ask this of us!"

I've been on that trail.
You've been on that trail.
And none of us *want* to be on that trail.

Now, when Abraham received the command
to sacrifice his son,
he didn't immediately leave for Mt. Moriah,
First, he had to cut wood.
This means he had time to think.

The journey to Moriah took three days.
This means he had more time to think.

When he and Isaac arrived at the mountain,
Abraham took the wood from the servants
who had accompanied them
and told them to wait at the trailhead
until they got back.

He packed the wood
on Isaac's shoulders.
They climbed the mountain.

More time to think.

The passage does not indicate
that Abraham pleaded with God.
Or that he bargained with God.
Or got angry with God.

Some see in this reticence an indication
that Abraham's faith was unquestioning.
That, already, Abraham had decided
to submit to God.
Even to the point
of sacrificing his own son.

But I read this passage
from the perspective of Sam's bedside.
And I do not find faith.
Or the lack of it.

Instead, I find hope.
A desperate hope.
Because God does not lay down teaser trails.
And the trail of hope does not end on Moriah.
It continues to a hill called Calvary.

Before Abraham removed the wood
from Isaac's back,

Christ had already planned
to carry the cross on his own shoulders.

Before the angel removed the knife
from Abraham's hand,
        Christ had already forged a lance
        for the centurion's grip.

The trail of faith begins in confusion.
But continues in hope.

And those who sow in tears
        will reap with joy.

STAY WHERE YOU ARE

He enjoined them not to depart from Jerusalem.
(Acts 1:4)

When Jesus closed the door on the carpenter shop
and hit the road north out of Nazareth,
it didn't take him long to reach the Sea of Galilee.

There, he drew a line in the sand
and dared others to follow him:

Sell what you have, then come follow me!
If you want to save your life, give it away!
Let the dead bury the dead!
Unless you renounce all your possessions,
you cannot be my disciple!

Again and again, Christ challenged people
to leave their way of life behind.
In doing so,
he filled their minds with big dreams.
Dreams of the Kingdom of God
       where the hungry are fed,
       the sick recover,
       the wounded get bandaged,

prisoners released,
tears wiped away
and death is but a bad dream.

Come, follow me and you'll see big things.
And you'll do big things.
Because God is my Father
and my Father is the God of Big Things!

A Kingdom of hope,
adventure
and last-minute rescues!

A Kingdom of open space,
open hearts
and open arms!

Don't you just love this part of the Gospel?
The Call to Discipleship.
The challenge to break out, break free
and follow the Lord
with nothing to hold you back?

Like the song
in the heart of a young woman
who turns her back
on the bling and glamour of society
to take the veil and live the Gospel

in a convent
in a slum,
in a school,
in a hospital;
     to live in sisterhood
     and solidarity
     in a poor country;
     in a country at war.

I'm talking about the rush
in the blood of a young man
who joins the Special Forces,
not of the army, but the priesthood.
To give his all,
to give his best,
to serve the Church
and save his country.

Don't you love this part of the Gospel?
The part that moves young people
to reach for the sky
and dream the Big Dreams of God?

Yet, this excitement and adventure
is but one dimension of the Call to Discipleship.

Eventually, "Come, follow me"
turns into "Stay where you are."

We hit this speed bump
in today's passage
when Jesus says:
"Stay in the city
until you are clothed
with power from on high."

With these words,
Jesus tells his followers to brace themselves.
      Where he is going, they cannot follow.
      For the time being,
      they must remain where they are.

Yes, there comes a time when,
Come, follow me
turns into,
Remain where you are.

No doubt, many saints have sailed the seas,
blazed trails through the jungles and swamps,
built hospitals in cities like Calcutta
and missions in Texas and California.

In a recent article, Dr. Tom O'Neal
discusses a different type of disciple,
one who remains quietly faithful
to his or her corner of the world.

He ponders folks who live in houses
with a garages full of bicycles
and a high-mileage vehicle in the driveway.

Folks who follow Christ,
not by heading down the road,
but by putting down roots.
            People who stay in one place long enough
            to sanctify it with stability and dependability.

Do you ever consider how important
you are to God's plan
right where you are?

In a society where
            commitment is optional
            and morality is more apt to be applied
            to animal rights
            than to college kids hooking up.

Our world hungers for stability.
For the sound of a family—*your* family—
singing Happy Birthday off-pitch.

Our world longs to catch the glint of light
from a rosary in the calloused hand
of a husband praying for his wife;

in the chaffed hand of a wife
praying for her husband.

I, for one, long to overhear
a conversation between a father and his son
as they tear down an engine
in the shop behind the house.

We long for these simple things.
And how magnificent is our God
who does big things in small places!

Places as small as your kitchen
and your child's bedroom.
        Places as plain
        as the school cafeteria
        or the meeting room
        in the basement of your church.

Christ lived most of His life
within 100 miles of Nazareth.
Population: 500 people.

Yet, his life in a small place
redeemed humanity and all of history.

Stay where you are.
Sanctify the home where you live,

the place you work,
the kitchen you clean
the bedroom where you pray.

"Save the world," says the Lord,
"by helping me save the world
where you live."

BRING DOWN THE WALLS!

Suddenly there came from the sky
a noise like a strong driving wind.
(Acts 3:2)

The Day of Pentecost commenced in fear.
But the Spirit transformed that fear.
      Into exuberance.
      And strength.

Pentecost started with fear but evolved into action.
      Locked doors shot open.
      Disciples flooded the streets.

      The Church proclaimed the power of God
      in shouts and yelps
      in many tongues and accents.

This year,
for this priest,
the Day of Pentecost
arrived a week early.

Last Sunday afternoon,
I drove to Our Lady of Guadalupe Church
for a "Jericho Walk."

I didn't know what to expect,
but it started with prayers in church.
Soon after, we became a river of people
flowing out into the streets.

Just like Pentecost.

Beneath a silk canopy edged in gold,
six men hoisted a platform
that held an altar and the Blessed Sacrament.

Like a dove,
the canopy flapped and fluttered in the wind.

Just like Pentecost.

The crowd processed down an alley.
We turned a corner.
Women, arms swaying,
dresses twirling,
danced before the Sacrament.

The Mysteries of the Rosary floated in the air.
Words from the Book of Psalms

crackled from speakers,
the mic stands
weighted down on the bed of a truck
with bags of concrete mix.

Young men blew shofars.
Cries sailed to God:
"Tear down the walls!"

¡Diós, baja las paredes! ¡Diós, baja las paredes!

Lord, flatten the barriers of sin and division!
Demolish the walls that divide
        husbands and wives,
        parents and children,
        Mexicans and Americans,
        citizens and immigrants.

Just like Pentecost!
A week early. And not a day too soon
in this political year
when politicians and pundits feed the country
with helpings of fear and arrogance,
anger, disdain and division.

But you and me?
We live, not on loaves of fear,
but on Bread that comes down Heaven!

And the air we breathe?
Nothing less than the wind of God's Spirit,
rushing down streets
where children play
and families work
to make ends meet.

Where prayers are prayed
in churches and kitchens and family rooms;
everywhere that Christians
lift up the hope
of a land
where all God's children
live in peace and security,
unity and love.

Come, Lord Jesus!
Send us your Spirit!

Like Pentecost!
Just like Pentecost!

IT'LL MAKE YOU CRY

"Simon, you see this woman at my feet?
I tell you, her many sins have been forgiven
because she has shown great love."
(Luke 7:44)

Her many sins. Forgiven. *All* of them.

Today's gospel is about forgiveness.
And that's good news
because forgiveness is a good word.

Forgiveness is a wonderful word.
> Until you have to *use* it.
> Until you have to *say* it.
> Until you yourself
> have to *put it into practice.*

Let's say your life's going along smoothly.
You're moving along just fine.
Then some bully comes along,
> throws a log in your path,
> and you stumble.

What do you do when that happens?
Well, you pick yourself up,
        get back on your feet
        and move on as best you can.

But the fall takes a toll.
Inside, you've been wounded.
You've taken a hit.
        And the only splint
        that's going to set that broken spirit,
                the *only* ointment
                that's going to numb the pain
                is forgiveness.

But the wound throbs tender.
Just the notion
of setting that bone,
        just the thought
        of smearing ointment
        on that open sore
        makes you wince.

Yes. Forgiveness *is* a wonderful word
until you have to apply it.

And that's just one side of forgiveness.

What about when the tables are turned
and *we're* the bullies?

When we're the ones
doing the tripping and causing the pain???

When we get caught,
what do we do?
When we get called out,
how do we respond?

Usually, when backed in a corner,
we swallow our pride,
clear our throats and say something like:
　　　"Sorry, pal.
　　　Didn't mean it.
　　　Honest.
　　　Forgive me, all right?"

That's what we do when we screw up and get caught.
　　　We cough up the words:
　　　I'm sorry. Please forgive me.
　　　Then set out to set things right.

But what about God?
What's God's "take" on the word forgiveness?

Interestingly enough,
　　　His perspective
　　　has nothing to do
　　　with waiting for apologies.

It reaches far beyond
conditions and restitution.
It has nothing to do
with wounded pride.

Rather, because it is a "God" thing,
forgiveness is a *deep* thing, meaning,
it has everything to do,
not with broken hearts
or broken promises,
but broken *lives.*

Just ask the woman in today's gospel,
the one with the mascara
running down her face.

Just ask King David,
caught with his pants down
and now facing a murder conviction.

Just ask St. Peter,
caught in a lie outside the jail
where soldiers prepare to torture
the best friend he's ever had,
the one he's just denied
ever setting his eyes on.

What's God's take on *forgiveness?*

You could ask that woman,
you could ask King David,
you could ask St. Peter.

But, it'd be better if you asked yourself.

So, go ahead, ask yourself:

How did it feel the last time
you did something
              so embarrassing,
              so humiliating
              so *unforgivable*
that the only response was to break down
and sob?

Uncontrollably.

If you're like me,
you don't want to think about *that part* of forgiveness.

The part when you lose control.
Throw in the towel.
Throw up the hands.
Give up and give in.

Or *Part B,*
when you stop sobbing,
regain composure
and patch things up.

But, here's the deal:
when it comes
to God's part of the equation,
        God doesn't ask for this.
        He doesn't expect it.

When it comes to his forgiveness,
God simply wants you to receive it.

Divine forgiveness.
Undeserved forgiveness.

St. Peter experienced it
the moment the rooster crowed
and his pitiful protests
echoed off the stone walls
of the Jerusalem Jail.

And he wept.

The woman with the jar of oil
experienced forgiveness

the night she crashed the party
at the home
of a man named Simon.

And she wept.

What about you?

Have you allowed God's forgiveness
to reach that deep?
Have you allowed God's mercy
to move you to tears?

Human forgiveness requires human effort.
But divine forgiveness is a pure gift.
A gift that none of us deserves.

When you're ready to receive it,
God will hand it to you.

And when he does,
you'll never be the same.

IDENTITY. INTIMACY. COMMUNION.

"Who do you say that I am?"
(Matthew 16:15)

Identity.
Personal identity.

In the past,
a person identified
with their neighborhood,
hometown,
local parish,
or their county.

But these days, group identity
gives way to personal identity.

One's personal *brand* is mighty important.

This also seems to be the Lord's concern
in today's passage.
He asks, "Who do people say that I am?"
Yet, he frames the question differently
than we do today.

The question beneath our personal profiles
—from e-Harmony to Facebook—
is not,
"Who do people say that I am?"
but rather,
"Do you like my image of myself?"

We become proficient at selling ourselves.
We know the essential components
and how to dress them up:
       physical features,
       likes and dislikes,
       friends and interests,
       attitudes and opinions.

These things define who we are.
They comprise our identity.
At least, our public identity.

This sounds similar to the public identity
about which Jesus inquires of his disciples:
       What are people saying about me?
       With whom do they compare me?
       Who do they say I am?

But then comes a second question.
With just one word,
Jesus changes the tone of the passage:
"Who do *you* say that I am?"

Suddenly, the focus shifts
from identity to intimacy.

Identity and intimacy are not the same.
        They are different.
        Very different.

The difference between public identity
and personal intimacy
        is the difference between
        what you read on Facebook
        and what you read
        in the eyes of your spouse of 30 years.

It is the difference
between what you see in a selfie
taken on some beach
and what you see in the expression
on the face of a stranger
in an ER waiting room at 2 AM.

The first skims the surface,
the other plunges deep.
One is superficial,
the other profound.

Who do *you* say that I am?
This is not a public question.

It is a private question
and we find it disconcerting.

Especially when we gather at church.
After all, this is a public place.
Therefore, we are conditioned
to respond in a public way.

Like fifth graders in English class,
we raise our hands and squirm in our seats:
"I know!
I know!
Call on me!"

Then we stand and answer the question with pride:
*You are the Messiah, the Son of God, born of the Virgin
Mary; who suffered and died and was buried and rose
from the dead and are seated at the right hand of God,
the Father Almighty and someday you will return to judge
the living and the dead.*

This is the correct answer.
For a public question.

It is admirable that we know the correct answer.
The public response is nothing less
than the Faith of the Church,
the Truth revealed by God.

But, according to biblical scholars,
the original meaning of the word, "believe,"
had nothing to do
with the recitation of doctrines and teachings.

Rather, in both the Latin and the Greek,
the term, *to believe,* means "to give one's heart."

This moves us, then,
from a public question
to an intimate answer:
Who do you say that I am?

With this question,
we're no longer talking identity.
We're talking intimacy.
And the Word of God today
challenges us
　　　　to dig beneath the skin,
　　　　through muscle and tendons,
　　　　blood and corpuscles.
　　　　Down to the deepest needs
　　　　of your soul.

If you are a farmer,
your answer will carry the feel of gratitude
for rain that falls on the soil of your field.

If you are a mother,
your answer will echo the song
you sing to your children at bedtime.

If you are a father,
your reply will surge like adrenaline
when danger threatens the family you love.

Why?
Because these are the things that comprise
the most important aspects of your life.
They form the very structure of your identity.
There is no intimate sharing
of your personhood
without them.

"Who do you say that I am?" asks the Lord.

When Christ asks you this question,
he means to reveal to you
the deepest elements of his own identity.

Can you grasp them?

Can you heft their weight
in the wooden beam
that bruised his shoulder?

Does his forgiveness,
muttered through swollen lips
and broken teeth,
loosen sin's grip on your throat?

Who is your God?
Who is your Lord?

The answer centers on intimacy.
Not identity.

Intimacy.

As encountered in honest repentance.

Spiritual intimacy.

As when battles are won
at the shout at of his Word.

When fear flees
and weakness turns to power.

> As in that moment
> when the Bread is broken
> and the Chalice
> rests heavy in your hand.

That moment when
the deepest part of you
communes
with the deepest part of God.

HAND TO THE PLOW

As they were going along the road,
someone said to him,
"I will follow you wherever you go."
(Luke 9:57)

I passed two fellows on bicycles.
They wore white shirts.
Backpacks bounced on their shoulders
as they peddled their way down the street.

Inside those backpacks were Bibles.
And I thought to myself,
I hope they're not headed to my door.

I don't waste time with proselytizers.
It's like pouring water into a glass that's already full.
Nothing gets in!

The next day,
I shared my opinion with a friend I'll call Bob.
But I used a different analogy.
I didn't compare evangelists

to glasses full of water.
Instead, I said it was like talking to a drunk.

As soon as I said it,
I wanted to stuff the words back into my mouth.

Bob, you see, is a recovering alcoholic.
Fortunately, he didn't take offense.
He just looked at me in a sad way and said,
"Gosh, Father, I look forward to their visits."

I put my hand on his shoulder.
"Bob, I had no idea you were *that* lonely."

We both laughed.
Then he asked:
"When those guys come to your door,
what do you talk about?"

"We don't talk. We argue."

"That's where you go wrong," Bob replied.
"When they come to my door,
we don't argue religion.
We talk about struggles.
I tell them about mine and ask about theirs."

FR. JIM SCHMITMEYER

Bob is a smart man.
He attended the School of Hard Knocks
and graduated at the head of his class.
He lost battles along the way.
But those battles brought him back to Christ
and back to the Catholic Church.

We don't talk religion, we talk about our pasts.

That statement says a lot about Bob.
Instead of running away from his past,
he accepts it, he embraces it.
He uses lessons from the past
to navigate his future.
He looks to the past
to determine what lies ahead.

How does Bob's approach
square with the message in today's gospel
where Jesus says,
"Those who put their hand to the plow
and keep looking back,
are unfit for the Kingdom of God?"

In another place, Jesus insists that,
unless you turn your back
on your family, including your parents,
you are not fit to be his disciple.

60

Is he saying that everything you are,
everything you've learned
and everyone you've ever loved
is to be left behind in the dust?

No.

He is simply saying that, to be a true disciple,
you need a sharp focus.
Your life must be focused
—like a laser—
on his Word and his Truth;
focused on his Vison for you
and the world around you,
a world in desperate need
of justice, peace and mercy.

We don't talk about religion. We talk about our pasts.

There are two ways of looking back on your life:
with regret or with gratitude.

Gratitude for the family you come from,
the circumstances you grew up in,
the blessings
—as well as the challenges—
that were handed to you.

This past is a part of you.
Your past is part-and-parcel of your life.
And it is part-and-parcel of the life
that Christ asks you to offer to Him.

Your one and only life.
Your incredible and amazing life.
Your fearful and courageous life.

The life that you offer to God today.
At this Mass.
On this altar.

The life which the Lord, himself,
receives into His hands with deep appreciation.

This is what He desires.
This is all that He desires:

     Your life in his hands.
       Your amazing life.
         Your one and only life.

GOD'S STORY

But a Samaritan had compassion on him,
and went to him and bound up his
wounds, pouring in oil and wine.
(Luke 10:33)

"Tell me about yourself."

How might you respond to that question?
If you're a teenager,
young adult,
or middle age,
you will tend to respond by saying,
"I'm a student."
Or "I'm an athlete."
Or "I'm a carpenter."
"A teacher."
"A dentist."

But if you ask someone who is retired,
you'll receive a different type of response.
The retired person will respond with a story:

"Who am I? Well, let me tell you.
My parents came from Mexico."

Or, "My grandparents emigrated from Germany."
Or, "I come from a family of horse traders."

Then the person will smile,
look off in the distance,
and continue speaking
as though reciting a poem:
"I grew up in Oklahoma.
Was baptized at Sacred Heart Church.
I graduated from Ardmore High School.
Got married.
Joe was a roustabout
and lost his arm in the oil field.
We lived in a yellow house on the edge of town.
Twelve years ago,
our son died in an auto accident.
I grieve for him to this day.
And this, my friend, is who I am."

You hear the difference.
One person identifies with their work.
The other person identifies with their history.
So, it would seem that,
the older and wiser we become,
the more we recognize our true identity
as part of a larger story.

WILDFIRE

What sort of story is shaping your life?
Who are the villains?
The heroes?

Seeing the events of your life within the arc
of a larger story,
reveals the deeper dimensions of your life.

> When individuals no longer see their lives
> as part of a great epic,
> they cease to experience life as a narrative
> imbued with purpose and meaning.

Without an overarching narrative,
life begins to resemble an endless loop
of satires, sit-coms and so-called reality TV.
This is tragic because,
without a story to define who we are,
ideals like goodness and nobility
fail to carry the day.

With no great story to inspire us as a nation,
the concept of justice-for-all does not prevail.

Without the narrative of Salvation,
human history holds no happy ending.

In short, we can't live a good life without a good story.

This is why the Church has always taught
that it is a grave sin to miss Sunday Mass.

> When we no longer participate
> in the narrative of Redemption,
> we abandon our role
> in the Great Story of God.

This abandonment robs individuals
of ultimate meaning.
It also diminishes
the public witness of the Church.

The result is that other stories
—dark and misleading—
fill the emptiness left behind.

Consider today's episode
of the Story of the Good Samaritan.

> Without this story of compassion,
> in which a despised foreigner
> tends to a stranger left for dead in a ditch,
> we would have no corrective vision
> to counter narratives of fear and suspicion.

WILDFIRE

Without stories of courage and risk,
we have no alternate perspective
to assess the unsettling events
that unfold around us each day:

In short, without God's Story to save us,
we have only the story of sin to destroy us.

So, thank God for the Story of God.
What an epic story it is!

In place of politicians whose actions proclaim,
"I am above the law,"
> Mary, the mother of Jesus proclaims,
> "I am the handmaid of the Lord."

In place of explosions and beheadings,
> we hear prophets announce a time
> when swords are beaten into plowshares
> and spears into pruning hooks.

Yes, thank God for God's Story!
The story wherein the Light of Christ
shines in the darkness.
And the darkness *shall not extinguish it*!

Each Sunday, the Book is opened.
The table is set.
And the Great Story of God is told yet again.

This story,
this story alone,
provides the world the truth that it seeks
and the hope for which it longs.

CHEAP GRACE

If your eye causes you to sin, gouge it out!
If your hand causes you to sin, cut it off!
(Matthew 5:29)

Did you catch that?
Gouge out your eye?
Chop off your hand?

Is this some Christian version of *sharia law?*

No. Of course not.
The Lord is speaking figuratively.
But this does not mean
that he is not speaking seriously.
His words are serious.
Deadly serious.
And he uses shocking figures of speech
to get our attention.

Torture.
Mutilation.
Foreshadowing his own Passion.

To grasp the underlying meaning,
it helps to approach this passage
in light of what he himself paid
to secure our redemption.

To appreciate the high cost of salvation,
consider two types of payment:
Cheap Credit vs. Hard Cash.

What is Cheap Credit?
A German seminarian, Dietrich Bonhoeffer,
drew attention to this concept during World War II.
He wrote that Cheap Grace (easy credit)
is similar to discount religion.

For instance,
when parents asks the Church to baptize their child,
then proceed to raise that child
in the Religion of Athletics,
such a baptism costs the parents nothing.

Cheap grace is at play
whenever we Catholics
make the Sign of the Cross over our hearts
but refuse to position that same Cross on our shoulder.

Let's say that you commit a sin:
>   You cheat on your spouse,
>   you cheat on your taxes,
>   you cheat on your tests.

>   You cheat the boss,
>   cheat the poor,
>   or cheat your kids.

Yet, you feel no need to confess your sins,
so you just absolve yourself and go your own way.

Cheap Grace is like buying a car from Fast Freddy.
It tells you that Jesus wants you to be happy.
No matter what.
Even when you've done something ugly.
It tells you that you are "saved" no matter what you do.

As one writer expressed it, cheap grace
>   "turns religion into a trinket,
>   removes the image of Christ from the Cross
>   and wipes all trace of blood from the wood."

What's the opposite of Cheap Grace?
Costly Grace.

St. Paul described it when he wrote,
"Your salvation was purchased at a staggering price."
This lead him to conclude
that true disciples must work out their salvation
"with fear and trembling."

Costly Grace is Christ asking his disciples,
"Can you drink of the cup of suffering
of which I am to drink?"

It is Christ requiring every disciple
to die to himself,
pick up the Cross
and follow in his steps.

It is Christ saying, "Sell what you have,
give the proceeds to the poor
then come, follow me."

It is Christ saying to each one of us today:
"If your eye causes you to sin, gouge it out!"

Conclusion:
Salvation is free. Discipleship is not.

And what is discipleship?

It is Christ calling a young woman or a young man
to forsake marriage and a family

in order to give themselves entirely to him
and to his Church.

Discipleship is Christ calling a husband to love his wife
in sickness and in health.
Depression, Parkinson's or Alzheimer's be damned!

Discipleship is Christ calling teenagers
to confront peers
who abuse the sacredness of sexuality.

It is Christ calling a family
to open its heart
to a child with special needs.

Why is this kind of grace so expensive?

Because Christ did not regard his own life
—his own skin—
too high a price to pay,
too deep a sacrifice to make
for our eternal life.

ALL SAINTS

Grant that we may work together for
the coming of your Kingdom
until the hour we stand before you,
saints among the saints in the halls of Heaven.
(Eucharistic Prayer for Reconciliation I)

Next week, the City of Amarillo
hosts the National Finals Ranch Rodeo.
Being Texans, we know the difference
between ranch rodeo
and professional rodeo.

In regular rodeo,
individuals compete against each other.
Ranch rodeo,
on the other hand,
is a team sport.

Both types of sports offer advantages.
But the unique value of a team sport
is the cooperation it teaches,
the mutual respect it builds,
the spirit of unity it forges
between the members of a team.

Today's Feast of All Saints
aims for the same goal.
It reminds us that, as members of the Church,
we are members of a team.

Today's event is as different from a regular saint's day
as Ranch Rodeo is distinct from the PBR.
It does not honor individual players
of high achievement and broad acclaim.
The names of the saints we honor today
do not appear in the Liturgical Hall of Fame.

Rather, the saints we honor today
are remembered by relatively few people,
usually just family members and good friends.

Yet, they are remembered nonetheless.
And, most importantly,
they are honored and loved by God
no less than the canonized saints
known to all the world.

You know some of the saints honored today:
        Your grandmother.
        Your grandfather.
        The uncle
        who helped you get your first job.
        The Sister of St. Francis
        who prepared you for First Communion.

The older brother
who went off to war and never came home.

This is their feast, the Feast of All Saints.
Yet, it is not just their feast.
It is our feast as well.

Why?
Because Christianity is more team sport
than individual competition.

As you know, St. Paul used athletic analogies
to describe the Christian life.

When he wrote about sin, for instance,
he borrowed a term from archery.
For Paul, sin meant "missing the mark."

His most famous athletic reference
concerned a marathon:
"The runners in the stadium all run the race,
but only one wins the prize.
Run, therefore, so as to win."

A marathon is not a team sport.
Still, I can't help but think that St. Paul
would appreciate next weekend's rodeo.
After all, he consistently urged Christians
to offer their lives as a sacrifice for others.

In other words,
to "take one for the team."

If one member suffers, all suffer.
If one member is honored, all rejoice.

So, on this Feast of All Saints,
imagine a crowd of fans
positioned alongside the final stretch:
saints who loved you
and continue to love you:
> your grandmother,
> your grandfather,
> your older brother.

Imagine them
> with smiles on their faces,
> shouts on their lips,
> towels in hand,
> bottles of water to quench your thirst.

Straining against the barriers!
Spurring you on to victory!

And waiting,
just waiting to take you in their arms again!

FLESH AND BLOOD

I am the living bread that came down from heaven.
(John 6:51)

When was the last time
you had to "get past" something
in order to move on?

Maybe you had to "get past"
the flippant remarks
of your teenager.
        The gloomy remarks
        of your depressed neighbor.
                The insult muttered
                by a subordinate at the office.

A similar dynamic occurs
in today's gospel reading.
In John's gospel, chapter six,
Jesus says again and again:
"My flesh is real food, my blood is real drink."

His listeners, many of them his own disciples,
are taken aback:

What's this guy talking about?
How can this man give us his flesh to eat?

But Jesus doesn't back down.
He doesn't backtrack.
He doesn't reply,
"Oh, forgive me, you misunderstood my intention.
I'm speaking figuratively here.
This Bread really isn't my Body,
it's just a *symbol* of my body."

That's not what he says
because that is not what he means.

Instead of easing the tone,
he cranks up the decibel.
In fact, he drives the point home
in a way that is hard "to get past."

You can't hear it in the English
but it is obvious in the original Greek.

First he says:
"Unless you eat my flesh, you shall not have eternal life."

The next time he says,
"Unless you *gnaw* on my flesh."

Yes, uses the word, *gnaw*.
Like a dog gnaws a bone.

A recent article by Lutheran pastor Nadia Bolz-Weber,
reflects on the grittiness of the Christian religion.

She expounds on elements of the Gospel
that are plain as dirt and hard as a fist:

The Messiah is born in a barn.
He spits in the dirt.
He fashions a whip.
He sweats blood.
He grits his teeth in agony.

Even after the Resurrection,
the Gospel remains physical:
Christ breaks bread in the village of Emmaus,
grills fish on the shore of Lake Galilee,
orders the apostle Thomas
to feel the ridges that scar his hands.

Pain and Violence.
Disease and Starvation.
Sin and Death.
These are physical realities.

Her ruminations on the Gospel
also highlight
the physical properties of the Sacraments.

You can't have a down-to-earth Gospel
suddenly turn all billowy
when it comes to the Eucharist.

My flesh is real food.
       Not just a notion.
       Not just an idea.

My blood is true drink.
       Not just a memory.
       Not just a flashback.

This belief in the True Presence of Christ
means that God *physically* places himself in our hands.
And this begs the question:

       Will we reverence him
       with the attentiveness of Mary,
       the virgin mother?

       Will we guard him
       with the diligence and devotion
       of Joseph?

Or treat him with the scorn
of a Roman soldier?

God is real.
God is tangible.
He walks this earth today
        in a body as skinny as that of a refugee;
        in a body scarred with shrapnel;
        in a body that stinks with infection.

Our God:
warm as flesh,
red as blood.

This is the difference between true communion
and symbolic communion.

And this difference makes all the difference.
All the difference in the world.

FATHER'S DAY

*A father's blessing strengthens the
houses of the children.*
(Sirach 3:9)

I pulled into Toot-n-Totum to gas up my truck.
It was 10 o'clock in the morning,
not many customers.

I'd just topped off my tank
when a gray pickup chugged off the street
and pulled to the air pump:
A work truck.
One fender coated in primer.
A dent in the tailgate.

What caught my attention more than the truck
was the presence of the driver's young son.

They checked the air pressure in a back tire.
They had the same walk and same build.
They both wore caps, tee-shirts and faded jeans.
Clearly, this apple did not fall far from the tree.

After they pulled away
I wished I had had a chance to talk with them
and learn a bit about their story.

I love stories about sons and dads.
I often wonder what sort of father I would have been
if fatherhood had been my calling.

When I was a kid, my favorite TV show was *The Rifleman,*
a story about a man and his young son
living in a cabin, living off the land.

This weekend is Fathers' Day.
Unfortunately, our entertainment industry
doesn't focus much on Fatherhood these days.

Even here in church, we don't talk much about fathers.

We learn that James and John were sons of Zebedee.
We hear about the son of Timeaus
whose sight was restored.
Peter himself is called Simon, son of Jonah.
    Yet we learn nothing about their fathers.
    Likewise, most of our male saints
    are priests, bishops and monks.

Yet, there are amazing fathers in the history of the Church,

St. Eustachius, for instance,
a Roman general under Emperor Trajan.
One day, flush from victory,
Eustachius and his troops marched into Rome.
Trajan held a public ceremony
but Eustachius refused to sacrifice animals
to the pagan gods,
thus exposing himself as a Christian.

Trajan immediately ordered the execution of the general
along with his wife and two teenage sons.

St. John Paul II once wrote that
every effort must be made
to restore the conviction that the work of the father
in, and for, the family
is unique and irreplaceable.

Today, we thank God for fathers we know and admire.
They come in many models
ranging from St. Eustachius
to the Rifleman,
to our own dads or step-dads.

Myself, I'm going to say an extra prayer
for the father I observed
pumping air into a tire at Toot-n-Totum.

I don't know his story.
I don't even know if he is a Christian.
But I'm going to pray for him.

Because he is a father.
And because, when he knelt to put air in the tire,
his son stood next him,
his hand on his dad's shoulder.

I don't know their story, but I know God's story.
A story about a Father.

A Father who loved his Son.
And a Son who loved his Father.

SONG OF LIFE

*Mary has chosen the better part, which
will not be taken away from her.*
(Luke 10:42)

A writer named John Sowers
recently described his family's visit to an aquarium.
His young daughters,
who love fish the way other children love puppies,
ran to the entrance
as though a Christmas tree
with a hundred gifts
waited inside
just for them.

Upon entering the aquarium,
the girls stood silent, transfixed by wonder.
        They leaned back
        to gaze at the bellies of sharks,
        were hypnotized
        by the flapping wings of stingrays,
        stood frozen in place
        beside a wall of blue coral.

But this was not the father's experience.
Watching his daughters,
he came to the conclusion that,
somewhere along the way,
he had gone tone deaf.
No longer able to hear the Great Music of Creation.

When did I stop hearing it? he asked himself.
Later, that night, he wrote this:

What closed me off?
What jaded me, made me cynical, doubtful and afraid?
Was it broken relationships?
Or the frantic pace I live,
reacting from one crisis to another crisis?
Was over-familiarity breeding contempt in my heart?

And then, he asked the hardest question of all:
Once someone stops hearing the music,
can they ever hear it again?

I wonder if Martha asked herself the same question,
late in the evening,
after Jesus had dined at her house
and gone back home.

As she dried the dishes
and put them back in the cupboard,
she must have realized,

like the father at the aquarium,
she, too, had missed the music.
> Anxious and irritable,
> she'd missed the concert
> while her sister, Mary,
> had enjoyed a front row seat.

"Martha, Martha," said the Lord,
"you are anxious and worried about many things.
Mary has chosen the better part
and it will not be taken from her."

How different our day-to-day grind if,
like children at an aquarium,
or Mary sitting at the feet of the Lord,
we could simply receive the gift of life
with gratitude and joy.

What would that world be like?
We might loosen our grip
on the need to be in control.

We might inventory blessings
instead of forebodings.

We would offer praise
in place of criticism.

According to Mr. Sowers,
we might even stop posting hateful comments
on the Internet!

Not to mention cutting down over-time at work,
changing the tone of our prayer,
or taking hold of the hand of someone we love
and gazing into their eyes.

How do we get back to living life
as opposed to simply enduring it?

Is the answer Yoga?
More fiber, less carbs?
A renewed membership
at a fitness club?

In today's gospel,
Mary discovered the answer
at the feet of the Savior.

That's all it took.
A quiet conversation
and a deep gaze.

Into the eyes of Christ.
The eyes of Love itself.
A Love-beyond-all-telling.

SKIN TIME

For everyone who asks receives, and
everyone who searches finds,
and for everyone who knocks, the door will be opened.
(Luke 11:10)

For Blaise and Bernadette

Children struggle to communicate.
>Some words are hard to pronounce.
>Sometimes, sounds and syllables
>get twisted up.

>And sometimes the results are amusing.

A young girl was convinced she could speak Spanish,
thanks to Dora the Explorer.
One day at a Mexican restaurant,
the waitress said "Gracias!"
And the little girl,
with all the confidence in the world,
replied: "Piñata!"

Even though adults and children
use the same vocabulary,
they speak a different language.
Some level of translation is required.

In a similar way,
adults who attempt
to communicate with God,
can find themselves in the place of a child.
        Stammering.
        Stuttering.
        Trying hard to be understood.

And, no matter how hard we try,
we can't seem to get our point across:

            We ask God for a raise at work,
            but get laid off instead.

            We ask God to help us pass an exam,
            but we end up failing the course.

            We ask God to take away our loneliness
            only to find ourselves
            spending each evening
            scanning Facebook
            and drinking too many glasses of wine.

So, when we hear the words of today's gospel:
Seek and you will find,
knock and the door will be opened to you,
we wonder,

> "Which word did I not pronounce correctly?
> What line did I put in the wrong place?
> Why do I not receive
> that for which I beg?"

An easy question to ask.
A hard question to answer.

So, with this in mind,
let's revisit the gospel passage
and focus on the very last line:

> *If you then, who are wicked, know how to give*
> *good gifts to your children, how much more will*
> *the Father in heaven give the Holy Spirit to those*
> *who ask him?*

After being told to "ask and you shall receive,"
this conclusion is *not* what we expect, is it?

This is *not* how we want the passage to end.

Rather, we want to get what we want.
If we don't,
we might just throw a tantrum!

But, if we calm down for a moment,
we might also discover an amazing revelation.

We might begin to grasp
that there is something more important in play
than that for which we pray.

That "something more important" is the Holy Spirit.

In other words,
the deepest answer to our prayer
is not *the thing* for which we pray,
but *the Holy Spirit*
who prompts us to pray for it in the first place.

What does this mean?
This means that the act of praying
is more than a *one-time asking*.
It is an *on-going trusting*.

Deep prayer isn't a child crying,
"Gimme! Gimme!"
It is a child crying,
"Hold me! Hold me!"

In today's passage,
Jesus widens the concept of prayer
from getting what we want,
to the experience of resting,

like a child,
in the arms of God.

To illustrate this mystery,
consider what neonatologists refer to
as "skin time."

If you have ever spent time
in an Intensive Care Unit for Newborns,
you likely know about *skin time*.

Myself, I learned about "skin time" two weeks ago
when my niece, Vickie,
gave birth to pre-mature twins.
With her permission,
I share with you something of her story.

Over the years, Vickie and her husband, Alan,
have lost a number of children through miscarriages.
This has caused them deep grief and heartache.
Yet, each time they find themselves expecting a child,
they pray.

They pray hard.
And if you asked them
why they pray
and keep on praying,
they would say,

"What else can we do?
We have no other option."

Well, this time,
their prayers were answered.
But not completely.
At least not yet.

The twins have arrived, but they are tiny.
So praying and pleading resumes.

But now, in addition to the prayers
that the babies survive,
there is "Skin Time."

When little ones arrive so early,
doctors give orders that they be held naked
—as soon as possible and as long as possible—
against the naked skin of their parents.

What happens next?

In my family, the next thing that happens
is the e-mailing of naked babies
to relatives and friends
all across the country!

So, last week,
when I saw those tender pictures,

WILDFIRE

then read this Sunday's gospel,
I caught a glimpse of the Holy Spirit,
a vivid image of close contact
between God
and the children he so loves.

A connection as warm and intimate
as premature babies
swallowed in the embrace of their parents.

Heart to Heart.
Spirit to Spirit.
Skin on Skin.

My friends,
this is what it means to rest
in the embrace of the Holy Spirit:
> no matter what life might throw at us,
> no matter what tragedies befall us,
> no matter what fears
> or worries assault us.

Our deepest prayer,
our most desperate prayer
is "Skin Time" with God.

> Like the "skin on skin" prayer of every parent
> who has ever held a helpless child.

Like the "skin on skin" prayer
of every soldier who has ever dragged
a wounded comrade out of the line of fire.

Like the "skin-on-skin" prayer of every life guard
who has ever dived into the deep
to save a swimmer gasping for breath.

When you, yourself, dive this deep into prayer,
        when you pray
        and pray
        and keep on praying,
        you're not asking your heavenly Father
        for a fish or an egg.
        You are asking to be held.

You are asking for a love
that will carry you
though the darkest night
and darkest despair.

A Love to carry you
all the way to Heaven.

Day by day.
Year by year.
Skin on Skin.

EMPTY CHAIRS

The one who ate my bread has lifted his heel against me.
(John 13:18)

Empty chairs.
No one likes an empty chair.

> Family meals.
> Family reunions.
> Family of faith.

No one likes an empty chair.

Today's gospel reading
takes place at the Last Supper.
And the words point us to an empty chair.
The place at the table
left vacant by Judas.

Today's gospel picks up
at the place
where Judas ducked out.

He has just left the Upper Room
and everyone is staring
at an empty place at the table.

Were there any "empty chairs"
at your last family gathering?

How uncomfortable was the sight
of that chair?

Did it speak of anger?
Did it testify to some long-ago hurt?
Did it carry an echo of loud words?
Or just silent rejection?

Empty chairs at a table
are hard to deal with.

Sometimes an empty chair is no one's fault,
which makes the absence hurt all the more:
> A car accident.
> A fatal illness.

Or the reason might simply be
that someone lives far away.
> Or can't get off work.
> Or afford the expense of travel.

Regardless of the reason,
an empty chair saddens the spirit.

So, too, when it comes
to the gathering of God's family
here at Mass.

Whether we're talking about empty chairs
at the table in your house
or empty pews in church,
the absence of someone you love
opens an emptiness in your heart.

Sadly, a person who chooses not to attend
a birthday party
or Easter dinner
or Sunday Mass
usually has no idea how much they are missed.

There have been times in my life
when I've missed important celebrations.
        I've missed birthdays.
        I've missed weddings.
        I've even missed funerals.
        And each time,
        I convinced myself
        that my presence was not important.
        So, a place remained empty.

I've come to realize that the emptiest place
was not at some table
at a wedding hall
or a funeral luncheon,
but in my outlook.

So, let's go back to the gospel
and take another look at that empty place
at the table of the Lord.

Perhaps Judas did us a favor.

His empty chair is a reminder.
A reminder that
the absence of self-worth
is the deepest absence of all.

A PLACE AT THE TABLE

When you hold a banquet, invite
the poor, the crippled, the lame, the blind.
(Luke 14:13)

Weddings are wonderful occasions.
Everyone loves a wedding.
But, for those hosting a wedding,
the celebration is quite expensive.

The average cost of a wedding in Amarillo, Texas
ranges from twelve to twenty thousand dollars.

This is one reason
I always inform engaged couples that,
as far as the Church is concerned,
the Sacrament of Marriage requires
only the presence
of a bride and groom,
two witnesses
and a priest or deacon.
>   That's it!
>   No charge.
>   No obligation.

Just two hearts open to the Lord
and the grace of the Sacrament.

The engaged couple always seems relieved
at hearing this news.
But only until I ask
how many homeless people
they intend to invite to the reception.

Their smiles turn into frowns.
"What are you talking about?" they ask.

Then I quote them today's gospel:
"When you throw a party," says the Lord,
"invite those whom everyone else overlooks."

Has anyone here ever attended a wedding
or a *quinceañera* where, at the head table,
we find street people,
> drug addicts
> and runaway teenagers
> enjoying huge helpings
> of brisket, *cabrito* and wedding cake?

No.
It's not something people generally do.

Does the Lord truly expect us to invite them?
How literally are we to interpret these words?

Let's go back to the passage
and inspect the text more closely.

When you hold a lunch or a dinner, says the Lord,
do not invite your friends or your brothers
or your relatives or your wealthy neighbors
in case they may invite you back
and you have your repayment.
Rather, when you hold a banquet,
invite the poor, the crippled, the lame, the blind;
blessed indeed will you be
because of their inability to repay you.
For you will be repaid in the resurrection of the just.

Is the Lord recommending this course of action
so we might feel *good*
about doing a good deed?

No.
Not at all.

First of all,
note that he is not asking us to write a check
or to make a donation.
Rather, he is asking us to "make room."

And "to make room" means
make room in your heart
for the forgotten people,
the throw-away people,
people who have no one
to hold in their arms at night.

Those who have no place to call home.
Those who sleep beneath bridges.
Those whose only relief
comes through the end of a needle
shoved into a vein.

Secondly, notice the emphasis
the Lord places on repayment.
These people can never repay you.

But *he* can and *he* will.

Sometimes he repays us
in ways we would never imagine.

This past week,
a parishioner invited me to join him for lunch
at Faith City Mission where he works.

As we ate chili, he told me a story
about a young man at the facility

undergoing detoxification.
My friend did not want to impose
on the young man.
But there was something
that kept drawing his attention
to this new resident.

Finally, one day after lunch,
he introduced himself.
"My name's Michael," he said. "How's it going?"

They exchanged small talk
and learned that they came
from the same town in Oklahoma.
Then they started naming people they knew.

The young man's mother had left the town
when he was very young.
She lost touch with her family
and never returned.

That's when Michael asked the young man his last name
and learned that the young man's father
was actually Michael's own brother!

The stranger he was talking to
turned out to be
his own nephew.

Within weeks,
the family convened a reunion.

Centuries ago,
when rabbis were asked how to determine
the exact time of dawn,
they would reply,
"A new day begins when enough light exists
to distinguish the face of a brother or sister
from that of a stranger."

So, a place must be set.
Room must be made
in our hearts
and in our lives.

Because, in the Body of Christ,
the stranger is your kin,
your blood.

Blood is thicker than water.

And the thickest blood of all
is the Blood of Christ.

FIG TREE

A man had a fig tree planted in his vineyard;
and he came looking for fruit on it and found none.
So he said to the gardener, "For three years
I have come looking for fruit on this fig tree."
(Luke 13:8)

Imagine buying a house
with a pecan tree in the backyard.
At the closing, your banker leans over and whispers,
"Oh, by the way, that pecan tree?
You don't own any of the pecans
until the mortgage is paid off."

Or, consider this:

The Farm Credit Agency offers you
a good interest rate
on a piece of farm ground.
At the closing, the owner, a religious fanatic,
inserts a clause into the contract.

He insists that, every seven years,
the entire crop
be donated to a charity of his choice.

And you say, WHAT???
This doesn't make sense!

And you would be right.
In the State of Texas,
unless we're talking mineral rights,
nobody has authority to tell you
what you can or cannot do
with your property
or its produce.

But the Law of Texas
is not the Law of Moses.

Listen to this verse from the Book of Leviticus:

*When you come into the land and plant all kinds of trees
for food, for three years the fruit from a tree must not
be eaten. Then in the fourth year all its fruit shall be set
apart for the Lord. Only in the fifth year you yourself may
eat of the fruit, says the Lord your God.*

This brings us back
to the scrawny fig tree
in today's gospel,
the one that failed to produce fruit
for three years.

The "three years" is significant.

Why?
Because the next year,
the *fourth year*,
the figs from that tree
—all the figs—
would be offered to God.

So, this story isn't about
agricultural production,
it's about religious tithing.

It's about making an offering,
a generous offering,
from the work of your hands
to the Lord.

Did that barren tree
eventually produce a yield of figs
for the Lord?

We don't know.
The Gospel of St. Luke,
remains mute on this point.

But, later, in this same gospel
we encounter another barren tree:
> the tree on which hangs
> a lousy, no-good thief.

Of all four gospel writers,
only St. Luke mentions that,
> on Calvary,
> crucified next to Jesus,
> hung a man
> whose life bore little, if any, fruit.

That is until that moment when,
in his agony,
he turned to Jesus and begged,
"Lord, remember me
when you come into your kingdom."

On hearing these words,
Jesus heard more than a cry of desperation.
He heard a confession of faith.

He turned his face
to the man
on that barren tree and said:
"Today, you will be with me in paradise."

One Gospel, two trees.

Two barren trees.

Not much different from the lives of many of us here.
　　　One more year, we say to ourselves,
　　　just one more year..
　　　　　I'll make more money.
　　　　　I'll make amends.
　　　　　I'll pay up and pay back whatever I owe.

But there comes a time
—call it the fourth year—
when we realize
that we owe the Lord,
not a portion of our produce,
but the entirety of our life.

That's what the good thief offered to God.
Not a promise to do better.
Not a bargain for more time.
　　　　But his life.
　　　　His very life.
　　　　Barren as it was.

Tradition has given the thief a name:
St. Dismas.
The man whose life bore no fruit
except in his last hour.
The moment when he gave his all to Christ.

His offering took place at Calvary
the same hour the Son of Man
offered his life in love to the Father.

At this hour,
at this Mass,
the Lord waits for us
to do the same.

BEND THE KNEE

He poured water into a basin and began
to wash the disciples' feet.
(John 13:5)

When I hear the story of the Last Supper,
of how Peter refused to allow Jesus
to wash his feet,
I think back to my childhood
and recall a boy
from a neighboring farm.

On the day that his sister was married,
Tony spent most the day
inside his parents' car
instead of the reception hall.
His shoes were too small
and his feet hurt too bad.
So he kept to the back seat.

Shoes were expensive
and farm boys ran barefoot all summer.
In planning the wedding,
Tony's parents failed to notice

how much he had grown
and how much
>   barnyard gravel
>   and pasture field baseball
>   affect a young boy's feet.

>   So, on the wedding day, as grownups danced
>   and friends played hide-and-seek,
>   Tony hid in the car.

When I hear the story of St. Peter
barefoot at the Last Supper
I think of Tony
barefoot at his sister's wedding.

Other times,
I think of a statue in a country church
named for St. Louis, King of France.

>   At the center of the high altar
>   stands a large statue of the saintly king:
>>   A crown on his head.
>>   Flowing robes
>>   that shimmer
>>   with specks of gold.
>>   Things one would expect to see
>>   on the statue of a king.

Yet, at the base of the image,
the king's feet are bare.
No shoes.
No boots.
No sandals.

The bare feet of this barefoot king
declared that Louis' own king
was Christ the King
who came to serve, not to be served.

Sometimes,
when I hear about St. Peter
at the Last Supper,
I think about St. Louis instead.

Yet, tonight,
as we recall the Lord's Last Supper,
our focus should not be feet,
> Not the bare feet of St. Louis.
> Not the bare feet of some farm boy.
> Not the feet of St. Peter himself.

Instead of feet,
we must think about knees.

He poured water into a basin
and began to wash the disciples' feet.

To perform this task,
Jesus bowed his head
and bent his knee.

In doing so,
he gave us an example of humility and service.

He also showed us
a profound posture of prayer.

There are many postures to assume
when engaged in prayer.
Some people meditate on a yoga mat.
Others praise God by waving their hands.

Yet there is no better prayer
than the bend-your-knee kind of prayer.

After the Lord bent his knees
to wash his disciples' feet,
how can it be otherwise?

Tonight, Christ illustrates that,
to kneel
is to join in solidarity
with those whose lives
are bent
into a similar position:

A maid
cleaning a bathroom floor.
A mechanic
fixing a flat tire.
A grandmother
planting potatoes in a garden.
A mother
slipping a shoe on the foot of her toddler.
A father
crouched on the sideline of a ball diamond.
A young man
proposing marriage.
A child
kneeling at the side of a dog hit by a car.
A son
kneeling at the grave of his mother.

In the seminary, they taught us that
kneeling is a sign of repentance.

They were wrong.

Kneeling is a sign of *love*.
The deepest love
the human heart can feel.
Quiet love.
Humble love.
Embodied in the bowing of the head
and the bending of the knee.

Tonight, Jesus gives us an example
of humble service.
He also gives us
a sure posture
for true worship.

For true worship
is humble love.
A love so deep
that one must bow the head
and bend the knee
to reach it.

CLUTTER

I consider everything as a loss in light
of knowing Christ Jesus.
I have accepted the loss of all things and I
consider all those things as so much rubbish.
(Philippians 3:8)

Eighty-four percent of American communities
contain storage units for rent.

If St. Paul were preaching today,
he might just take us to one of those places
to drive home his message that,
in light of knowing Christ,
everything else just clutters up life.

So, let's imagine St. Paul
taking us on a field trip to a storage unit.
        He punches in a security code,
        rolls up a metal door
        and invites us inside for a look around.

He gives a broken down recliner a good kick.
Writes his initials in the dust on a flat-screen TV.

His concern is not the used furniture.
Rather, it's the time we waste
with a remote control in one hand.

And a beer in the other.

Off in the corner stands a worn-out desk.
A perfect symbol of your dead-end job.
Your employment pays the bills
but offers no other meaning or purpose.

Or joy.

Propped against the back wall,
a tattered mattress.
A testament to a time in your life
when your soul was empty
but your weekends were full.

Of one-night stands.

So, with St. Paul at our side,
we stare in silence
at all the junk in our life.

He crosses his arms and mutters,
"Rubbish."
Paul shakes his head then walks toward the door,

leaving us alone
surrounded by clutter.

Truth be told,
we wish we could just turn
and walk away
like St. Paul.
        Brush our hands
            of accumulated regret,
            past pride
            and threadbare comforts.

But we can't.
At least, that's how it feels.

Just how does someone
leave behind
the junk
that clutters life
and chains the soul?

To tackle that question,
consider the insight of St. Ignatius of Loyola.
In the 1600's, he wrote *The Spiritual Exercises*,
a work that includes this prayer:

Take, Lord, and receive all my liberty,
my memory, my understanding and my entire will;

all that I have and possess.
You have given all to me.
To you, O Lord, I return it.
All is yours, do with it whatever you wish.
Give me Your love and Your grace,
for this is enough for me.

This prayer urges the same spirit of detachment
found in today's passage from St. Paul.
But the prayer of Ignatius goes one step further.

It gives us a word,
a single word
        to serve as a pry bar
        to wedge open the door
        of every cluttered garage
        and crowded storage unit in town.

That word is *enough*.

"Give me only your love and your grace."

This is enough.
This is more than enough.

There is great freedom that comes from
dedicating all that we have to God.

We know this,
but no one is going "to give it all away"
      until they are convinced
        that they can retain what they need.

When will that occur?
When will enough be enough?

Someone once said
that the fear of not having enough
      is actually the fear
        of not being enough.

Are you enough?

If you consider yourself
lacking in some deep-down way,
it helps to remember
how God looks upon you.

This brings us to yet another saint, Augustine,
who once noted that,
when God gazes upon you,
it is as though no one else
in the universe exists!

Think on this:

FR. JIM SCHMITMEYER

In all of history,
there will never be another *you.*

No other human being
will ever have
the same mixture of emotions,
memories,
intellect,
talents,
skills,
and personality.

There will never be another person
on the face of this earth
who will sing and dance,
work and play,
laugh and cry,
discover, explore, create...
and love the way you do.

Take, Lord, and receive all that I have...
for it all comes from you!
Give me Your love and Your grace,
for this is enough for me.

God does not make junk.
God does not create clutter.

He created you.
And He loves you.
And in His eyes
you are enough.

In God's eyes
you are more than enough.

GOD'S DIAMOND

"Rejoice with me because I have
found the coin that I lost."
(Luke 15:9)

Have you lost anything lately?

What have you recently misplaced?
    Car keys?
    The TV remote control?
    Your I-phone?

These are small items that,
when misplaced,
cause a lot of frustration.

Usually, within a short time,
we recover the missing item
and life returns to normal.

Today's gospel passage
contains three parables about lost things:
    The Lost Sheep
    The Lost Coin
    The Lost Son.

Of the three missing items,
the middle story
—the one about the lost coin—
centers on an incidental item
       similar to our misplacing
       a set of keys
       or a remote control.

No big deal.
A quarter fell out from a woman's purse.
It's just a coin.
Some Bibles translate the word as "dime."

Perhaps this is why,
when we come across these three parables,
we focus on the Lost Sheep
or the Lost Son.
We seldom hear homilies
about the Lost Coin.

After all, it's hard to relate to a story
about a woman
who throws a party
to celebrate the fact that
she found a dime
       in a pile of dust
       when she swept the floor
       beneath the bed.

But this parable is about more
than finding a lost dime.

To better appreciate its message,
it helps to substitute
"engagement diamond"
or "wedding ring"
in place of the term
"lost coin."

In the ancient Mideast,
brides adorned themselves
with crowns dangling with sparkling coins.
If a wedding crown
lost one of its coins,
it would be similar to losing a stone
from a set of diamonds
in an engagement ring.

A small item.
But an item of tremendous value.

Without that coin,
the entire crown is marred
because it is incomplete.

The story about the Lost Coin, therefore,
plays a central role in

"The Lost Sheep-
Lost Coin-
Lost Son Trilogy."

The Lost Coin helps us realize
that each story
is about more than something lost.
Each story is about *life itself*
being incomplete.

This theme reaches its climax
in the final story when,
even after the Lost Son returns home,
the father is not at peace
until the Elder Son returns to the table.

>Without both sons beneath his roof,
>his heart remains broken
>and his family incomplete.

The parable about the lost coin
isn't talking about things like
car keys, remote controls or I-phones.
>It's about diamonds.
>And *you* are God's diamond.

Unless you suffer from narcissism,
it's hard to believe that,

in God's eyes,
you are indeed a diamond.

An honest look in the mirror,
any deep pondering of
        your life,
        your actions,
        your history,
        convinces you
        that you are a load of caliche,
        not a 10-karat diamond.

Just a pile of Dirt,
Gravel
and Grit.

In theological language,
we call it Sin.
Original Sin.
Sin with a capital "S."

And Sin and Diamonds don't fit together.

        Sin is the reason diamond rings
        end up in pawn shops.

        Sin is the reason life
        is a ride in a dump truck,
        not a sail boat.

WILDFIRE

Sin is the reason
you're more comfortable
being lost than being found.

But what can you do about it?

Nothing!
Left to our own devices,
we can *never escape*
the effects
of Adam's Sin.

Now and then,
we might experience a brief reprieve.
But, at the end of the day,
life is hard
and Sin wins out:

Friends let us down.
Family members turn on us.

We never reach our full potential.
Our fondest dreams
remain no more than dreams.

Just dreams.

In the midst of the disappointment,
resentment moves into our house
and sours the very air that we breathe.

Gravel and grit
on a county road.

And we know it.

But this is not how Christ sees us.
In his eyes, we are diamonds.

For this reason,
and this reason alone,
Christ descended to Earth,
    wore a crown of thorns,
    gave his back to the whip
    and stretched out his arms
    on the wood of the cross.

    This love,
    and this love alone,
    frees us from the power of Sin.

Why this extreme
"search and rescue effort"
on the part of God?

Because Sin (with a capital "S")
is far more serious
than the bad actions we commit
and the destructive words we speak.

The power of Sin
is more akin to an addiction
in which we are stuck.

Like a mouse on a glue trap.
And thrashing about
only makes it worse.

We have only to look at the story of humanity
and its vain attempts to save itself
to know the gravitational pull of Sin:
War.
Violence.
Slavery.
Oppression.

Face it.
We can no more save ourselves
than a mouse can escape
glue on a trap.

So, any rescue effort from the grip of Sin
must come from *outside of us*

and, at the same time,
enter deeply *into* us,
if we are to be delivered from its trap!

This is what happened on Calvary
when Christ sacrificed his life on the Cross.

> The liberating effects
> of that Sacrifice flow into the world anew
> each time you and I
> offer the Sacrifice of the Mass.

Why did Christ do this?
Why did he give his life on the Cross?

To retrieve a *diamond.*

A recent article by Bishop Robert Barron
cited ancient words of St. Anselm
who described the Son of God
diving to the murky bottom
of humanity's misery
to recover a diamond!

When the Savior rose,
the slime had been washed
from the precious stone.
The gem gleamed
with its original shine.

"Come, friends," shouts the woman
with a broom in hand
at the door of her house.
"Let's celebrate.
I've found my diamond!"

Today
we praise God
for finding us!

       "You are my diamond!" cries the Lord.
       "You are *my* diamond!"

Made in the USA
San Bernardino, CA
25 November 2016